50 German Cake Recipes

By: Kelly Johnson

Table of Contents

- Schwarzwälder Kirschtorte
- Bienenstich
- Frankfurter Kranz
- Donauwelle
- Käsekuchen
- Apfelstrudel
- Streuselkuchen
- Marmorkuchen
- Sachertorte
- Zwetschgenkuchen
- Baumkuchen
- Butterkuchen
- Rhabarberkuchen
- Käsekuchen mit Mandarinen
- Nusskuchen
- Kalter Hund
- Obstboden

- Linzer Torte
- Rote Grütze Kuchen
- Zitronenkuchen
- Heidelbeerkuchen
- Kirschstreuselkuchen
- Russischer Zupfkuchen
- Mohnkuchen
- Schmandkuchen
- Eierlikörkuchen
- Gugelhupf
- Quarkkuchen
- Pflaumenkuchen
- Marzipankuchen
- Buttercremetorte
- Haselnusskuchen
- Karottenkuchen
- Grießkuchen
- Vanillekuchen
- Topfkuchen

- Mandelkuchen
- Johannisbeerkuchen
- Puddingkuchen
- Zimtkuchen
- Streusel-Mohn-Kuchen
- Kirschtorte
- Eierkuchen
- Lebkuchenkuchen
- Holunderblütenkuchen
- Schokoladenkuchen
- Käsesahnetorte
- Früchtebrotkuchen
- Rosinenkuchen
- Torte mit Baiser

Schwarzwälder Kirschtorte (Black Forest Cake)

Ingredients:

- Chocolate sponge cake (3 layers)
- 600 ml heavy cream
- 3 tbsp sugar
- 1 tsp vanilla extract
- 2 tbsp cornstarch
- 700 g sour cherries (jar)
- 3 tbsp Kirschwasser (cherry schnapps)
- Chocolate shavings
- Maraschino cherries

Instructions:
Drain cherries, saving 200 ml juice. Thicken juice with cornstarch, stir in cherries, and let cool.
Whip cream with sugar and vanilla until stiff.
Sprinkle sponge layers with Kirschwasser.
Spread cherries over the bottom layer, then whipped cream.
Repeat for the second layer and top with the final sponge.
Cover the entire cake with whipped cream, decorate with chocolate shavings and cherries.
Chill before serving.

Bienenstich (Bee Sting Cake)

Ingredients:

- **Dough:** 250 g flour, 1 egg, 60 g sugar, 40 g butter, 125 ml milk, 1 tsp yeast
- **Topping:** 100 g sliced almonds, 75 g butter, 75 g sugar, 2 tbsp honey
- **Filling:** 500 ml milk, 40 g sugar, 1 packet vanilla pudding powder, 200 g butter

Instructions:
Mix dough ingredients, knead well, and let rise for about an hour.
Spread dough in a greased baking pan, let rise again.
Gently simmer topping ingredients until golden, then spread on the dough.
Bake at 180°C (350°F) for 25–30 minutes.
Cook vanilla pudding, let cool, and beat with butter.
Cut cake in half horizontally, spread the cream filling, and reassemble.

Frankfurter Kranz (Frankfurt Crown Cake)

Ingredients:

- 250 g butter, 250 g sugar, 5 eggs, 250 g flour, 2 tsp baking powder
- **Filling:** 500 ml milk, vanilla pudding powder, 250 g butter, 100 g sugar
- **Topping:** Red currant jelly, caramelized nuts or brittle

Instructions:
Make the batter with butter, sugar, eggs, flour, and baking powder.
Bake in a greased Bundt pan at 175°C (350°F) for about 45 minutes. Let cool and slice into 3 layers.
Cook the pudding, cool, and beat with butter and sugar.
Spread jelly and cream between layers, then frost the outside with the cream.
Decorate with brittle and rosettes of cream.

Donauwelle (Danube Wave Cake)

Ingredients:

- 250 g butter, 200 g sugar, 4 eggs, 375 g flour, 2 tsp baking powder, 2 tbsp cocoa powder

- 1 jar sour cherries, drained

- **Buttercream:** 500 ml milk, 1 packet vanilla pudding, 200 g butter

- **Topping:** 200 g dark chocolate

Instructions:
Make the batter, divide into two. Spread the light batter into a pan, then the cocoa batter on top.
Place cherries evenly, pressing slightly into the batter.
Bake at 180°C (350°F) for about 35 minutes.
Prepare the pudding, let cool, beat with butter.
Spread buttercream over cooled cake, chill.
Melt chocolate and pour on top. Allow to set before slicing.

Käsekuchen (German Cheesecake)

Ingredients:

- **Crust:** 200 g flour, 100 g butter, 50 g sugar, 1 egg

- **Filling:** 750 g Quark (or ricotta), 200 g sugar, 3 eggs, 1 packet vanilla pudding powder, 100 ml milk

Instructions:
Combine crust ingredients and press into a greased springform pan.
Mix filling until smooth and pour over the crust.
Bake at 170°C (340°F) for 60 minutes. Turn off oven and let cool slowly.
Chill well before serving.

Apfelstrudel (Apple Strudel)

Ingredients:

- **Dough:** 250 g flour, 1 egg, 1 tbsp oil, warm water as needed

- **Filling:** 5–6 apples, 50 g sugar, 1 tsp cinnamon, 50 g raisins, 50 g breadcrumbs, 50 g butter

Instructions:

Mix dough and knead until smooth and elastic. Let rest covered for 30 minutes.
Roll out very thin on a cloth.
Sauté breadcrumbs in butter.
Slice apples, mix with sugar, cinnamon, and raisins.
Spread breadcrumbs on dough, top with apples.
Roll up using the cloth, brush with butter.
Bake at 190°C (375°F) for 35–40 minutes. Dust with powdered sugar.

Streuselkuchen (Crumb Cake)

Ingredients:

- **Dough:** 300 g flour, 150 ml milk, 60 g sugar, 60 g butter, 1 egg, 1 tsp yeast

- **Streusel:** 200 g flour, 100 g sugar, 150 g butter, cinnamon (optional)

Instructions:
Prepare the yeast dough and let it rise for about an hour.
Spread in a baking tray, allow to rise again for 30 minutes.
Combine streusel ingredients into large crumbs, sprinkle over dough.
Bake at 180°C (350°F) for 30–35 minutes.

Marmorkuchen (Marble Cake)

Ingredients:

- 250 g butter, 250 g sugar, 5 eggs, 375 g flour, 1 packet baking powder, 4 tbsp milk, 2 tbsp cocoa powder

Instructions:

Cream butter and sugar, beat in eggs one by one.
Add flour and baking powder, alternating with milk.
Pour two-thirds of batter into a greased Bundt pan.
Mix cocoa into remaining batter and swirl it in.
Bake at 180°C (350°F) for about 60 minutes.

Sachertorte

Ingredients:

- 150 g dark chocolate
- 150 g butter
- 100 g powdered sugar
- 6 eggs (separated)
- 130 g granulated sugar
- 150 g flour
- Apricot jam
- **Glaze:** 200 g dark chocolate, 150 ml heavy cream

Instructions:
Melt chocolate and let cool slightly. Cream butter and powdered sugar, add egg yolks and melted chocolate.
Beat egg whites with sugar until stiff, fold into chocolate mixture with flour.
Pour into springform pan and bake at 170°C (340°F) for about 50–60 minutes.
Cool completely, cut in half, fill with warm apricot jam.
For the glaze, melt chocolate with cream and pour over cake. Let set before serving.

Zwetschgenkuchen (Plum Cake)

Ingredients:

- **Dough:** 300 g flour, 1 egg, 75 g sugar, 75 g butter, 150 ml milk, 1 packet yeast
- 800 g fresh plums, halved and pitted
- Optional: Streusel topping

Instructions:
Make yeast dough, let rise until doubled.
Roll out on a greased tray. Arrange plums closely in rows, cut side up.
Add optional streusel topping.
Bake at 180°C (350°F) for 30–40 minutes.
Best served with whipped cream.

Baumkuchen (Tree Cake)

Ingredients:

- 250 g butter
- 250 g sugar
- 6 eggs
- 100 g marzipan
- 100 g flour
- 100 g cornstarch
- 1 tsp vanilla extract
- 2 tbsp rum
- **Glaze:** dark chocolate

Instructions:
Cream butter, sugar, eggs, and marzipan until smooth.
Add flour, starch, vanilla, and rum.
Grease a springform pan. Spread a thin layer of batter and grill or broil until golden.
Repeat with several thin layers until batter is used.
Cool and coat with chocolate glaze.

Butterkuchen (Butter Cake)

Ingredients:

- 500 g flour
- 200 ml milk
- 75 g sugar
- 1 egg
- 75 g butter (for dough), plus 100 g for topping
- 1 packet yeast
- 100 g sugar (for topping)
- Sliced almonds

Instructions:
Make yeast dough and let rise.
Roll out on baking tray. Dot with butter pieces, sprinkle with sugar and almonds.
Let rise 15 more minutes.
Bake at 200°C (390°F) for 20–25 minutes.

Rhabarberkuchen (Rhubarb Cake)

Ingredients:

- 500 g rhubarb, peeled and chopped
- 200 g flour
- 100 g butter
- 100 g sugar
- 2 eggs
- 1 tsp baking powder
- Optional: meringue topping or streusel

Instructions:
Cream butter and sugar, add eggs. Mix in flour and baking powder.
Spread into a greased pan, top with rhubarb.
Add streusel or meringue if desired.
Bake at 180°C (350°F) for 35–40 minutes.

Käsekuchen mit Mandarinen (Mandarin Cheesecake)

Ingredients:

- **Crust:** 200 g flour, 100 g butter, 50 g sugar, 1 egg

- **Filling:** 750 g Quark or ricotta, 200 g sugar, 3 eggs, 1 packet vanilla pudding powder, 100 ml milk, 1 can mandarin oranges

Instructions:

Prepare crust and press into springform pan.
Mix filling ingredients and fold in drained mandarins.
Pour filling onto crust.
Bake at 170°C (340°F) for 60 minutes. Cool and chill before serving.

Nusskuchen (Nut Cake)

Ingredients:

- 250 g butter
- 200 g sugar
- 4 eggs
- 300 g flour
- 1 packet baking powder
- 200 g ground hazelnuts or walnuts
- 100 ml milk

Instructions:
Cream butter and sugar, beat in eggs.
Add flour, baking powder, and milk.
Stir in ground nuts.
Pour into loaf pan and bake at 175°C (350°F) for 50–60 minutes.

Kalter Hund (No-Bake Chocolate Biscuit Cake)

Ingredients:

- 200 g coconut oil or butter
- 200 g dark chocolate
- 2 eggs (optional)
- 100 g powdered sugar
- 200 g plain butter biscuits

Instructions:

Melt chocolate with coconut oil. Beat eggs with sugar, stir into chocolate (if using).
Line loaf pan with parchment paper.
Layer biscuits and chocolate mixture alternately.
Chill for several hours or overnight.
Slice cold.

Obstboden (Fruit Flan)

Ingredients:

- 150 g flour
- 75 g sugar
- 75 g butter
- 2 eggs
- 1 tsp baking powder
- Mixed fresh fruits (berries, kiwis, peaches, etc.)
- Clear cake glaze

Instructions:
Mix ingredients to form sponge base, bake in flan tin at 180°C (350°F) for 20–25 minutes.
Cool, flip onto plate.
Top with sliced fruit.
Prepare glaze as directed and pour over fruit. Chill before serving.

Linzer Torte

Ingredients:

- 200 g flour
- 100 g ground hazelnuts or almonds
- 150 g butter
- 100 g sugar
- 1 egg
- 1 tsp cinnamon
- 1 pinch cloves
- 200 g red currant or raspberry jam

Instructions:
Mix dough ingredients and chill for 30 minutes.
Press most of the dough into a tart pan. Spread with jam.
Roll out remaining dough, cut strips, and lay in lattice over jam.
Bake at 180°C (350°F) for 30–35 minutes. Let cool before serving.

Rote Grütze Kuchen (Red Berry Pudding Cake)

Ingredients:

- **Base:** 200 g flour, 100 g butter, 75 g sugar, 1 egg

- **Pudding layer:** 500 ml milk, 1 packet vanilla pudding powder, 2 tbsp sugar

- **Topping:** 500 g mixed red berries, 2 tbsp cornstarch, 2 tbsp sugar

Instructions:
Make crust, press into a springform pan, and pre-bake for 10 minutes at 180°C (350°F).
Cook pudding and spread over crust.
Simmer berries with sugar and cornstarch until thickened, let cool slightly, and spread over pudding.
Chill before serving.

Zitronenkuchen (Lemon Cake)

Ingredients:

- 250 g butter
- 250 g sugar
- 4 eggs
- 300 g flour
- 1 packet baking powder
- Zest and juice of 1 lemon
- **Glaze:** Powdered sugar + lemon juice

Instructions:
Cream butter and sugar, add eggs, lemon zest, and juice.
Mix in flour and baking powder.
Bake in loaf pan at 175°C (350°F) for 50–60 minutes.
Cool slightly, glaze with lemon icing.

Heidelbeerkuchen (Blueberry Cake)

Ingredients:

- **Dough:** 250 g flour, 125 g butter, 1 egg, 75 g sugar
- 400 g fresh or frozen blueberries
- Optional: 1 tbsp sugar + 1 tsp starch for berries

Instructions:
Make shortcrust dough, chill, and press into tart pan.
Sprinkle berries with starch and sugar, spread over base.
Bake at 180°C (350°F) for 30–35 minutes.
Dust with powdered sugar before serving.

Kirschstreuselkuchen (Cherry Crumb Cake)

Ingredients:

- **Base:** 300 g flour, 1 packet yeast, 100 ml milk, 50 g sugar, 50 g butter, 1 egg
- 1 jar sour cherries, drained
- **Streusel:** 200 g flour, 125 g butter, 100 g sugar

Instructions:
Prepare yeast dough, let rise.
Roll out on a baking tray, top with cherries.
Mix streusel ingredients into coarse crumbs and scatter over cherries.
Bake at 180°C (350°F) for 30–35 minutes.

Russischer Zupfkuchen (Russian Pluck Cake)

Ingredients:

- **Chocolate dough:** 300 g flour, 200 g butter, 125 g sugar, 40 g cocoa powder, 1 egg

- **Filling:** 500 g Quark or ricotta, 200 g sugar, 3 eggs, 1 packet vanilla pudding powder, 100 g butter

Instructions:
Mix dough and press 2/3 into springform pan (bottom and sides).
Prepare filling and pour in.
Tear remaining dough into chunks and "pluck" over top.
Bake at 180°C (350°F) for 50–60 minutes. Cool completely.

Mohnkuchen (Poppy Seed Cake)

Ingredients:

- **Dough:** 250 g flour, 125 g butter, 1 egg, 75 g sugar

- **Filling:** 500 ml milk, 100 g sugar, 1 packet semolina pudding or starch, 200 g ground poppy seeds

Instructions:
Make dough, chill, and roll into tart pan.
Cook milk with pudding powder and sugar, stir in poppy seeds.
Spread filling over crust.
Bake at 180°C (350°F) for 35–40 minutes. Dust with powdered sugar.

Schmandkuchen (Sour Cream Cake)

Ingredients:

- **Crust:** 250 g flour, 125 g butter, 75 g sugar, 1 egg

- **Filling:** 400 ml milk, 1 packet vanilla pudding, 3 tbsp sugar, 400 g Schmand or sour cream

- Optional: Fruit layer (apricots, peaches, etc.)

Instructions:
Prebake crust at 180°C (350°F) for 10 minutes.
Cook pudding and let cool slightly. Stir in sour cream.
Spread filling over crust, add optional fruit, and bake for another 25–30 minutes.
Chill before serving.

Eierlikörkuchen (Egg Liqueur Cake)

Ingredients:

- 250 g powdered sugar
- 5 eggs
- 250 ml Eierlikör (advocaat/egg liqueur)
- 250 ml neutral oil
- 250 g flour
- 1 packet baking powder

Instructions:

Mix eggs and powdered sugar until fluffy.
Add oil and Eierlikör gradually.
Fold in flour and baking powder.
Pour into greased Bundt pan and bake at 175°C (350°F) for 50–60 minutes.
Optional: glaze with Eierlikör icing or powdered sugar.

Gugelhupf

Ingredients:

- 250 g butter
- 200 g sugar
- 5 eggs
- 300 g flour
- 1 packet baking powder
- 100 ml milk
- Optional: 100 g raisins soaked in rum, 50 g chopped almonds

Instructions:
Cream butter and sugar, add eggs one at a time.
Mix in flour and baking powder, then add milk.
Fold in raisins and almonds if using.
Pour into greased and floured Gugelhupf pan.
Bake at 175°C (350°F) for 50–60 minutes. Dust with powdered sugar after cooling.

Quarkkuchen (German Cheesecake)

Ingredients:

- **Crust:** 200 g flour, 100 g butter, 50 g sugar, 1 egg

- **Filling:** 750 g Quark or ricotta, 200 g sugar, 1 packet vanilla pudding powder, 3 eggs, 100 ml milk, zest of 1 lemon

Instructions:
Make crust and press into a springform pan.
Mix filling ingredients and pour into crust.
Bake at 170°C (340°F) for 60–70 minutes.
Cool completely and chill before serving.

Pflaumenkuchen (Plum Cake)

Ingredients:

- 300 g flour
- 1 packet yeast
- 100 ml milk
- 50 g sugar
- 1 egg
- 75 g butter
- 800 g plums, halved and pitted
- Optional: Streusel topping

Instructions:
Make yeast dough and let rise until doubled.
Roll out onto a tray, top with plums.
Add streusel if desired.
Bake at 180°C (350°F) for 30–40 minutes. Serve with whipped cream.

Marzipankuchen (Marzipan Cake)

Ingredients:

- 200 g marzipan
- 200 g butter
- 150 g sugar
- 4 eggs
- 200 g flour
- 1 packet baking powder
- 50 ml milk

Instructions:
Grate marzipan. Cream with butter and sugar, add eggs.
Mix in flour and baking powder, add milk to loosen batter.
Pour into loaf or springform pan.
Bake at 175°C (350°F) for 50–60 minutes. Dust with powdered sugar or glaze.

Buttercremetorte (Buttercream Layer Cake)

Ingredients:

- **Sponge:** 6 eggs, 180 g sugar, 150 g flour, 50 g cornstarch

- **Buttercream:** 500 ml milk, 1 packet vanilla pudding powder, 2 tbsp sugar, 250 g butter

Instructions:
Bake sponge in springform pan at 180°C (350°F) for 25–30 minutes. Cool and slice into 2–3 layers.
Cook pudding and let cool. Beat butter until fluffy, slowly add pudding.
Layer cake with buttercream, cover outside, and decorate with nuts or chocolate shavings. Chill well.

Haselnusskuchen (Hazelnut Cake)

Ingredients:

- 250 g ground hazelnuts
- 250 g sugar
- 4 eggs
- 100 g flour
- 1 tsp baking powder
- Optional: 100 ml milk or cream

Instructions:
Beat eggs and sugar until fluffy.
Fold in hazelnuts, flour, baking powder, and milk if needed.
Pour into greased pan and bake at 175°C (350°F) for 50 minutes.
Dust with powdered sugar or cover with chocolate glaze.

Karottenkuchen (Carrot Cake)

Ingredients:

- 300 g grated carrots
- 200 g flour
- 150 g sugar
- 4 eggs
- 100 ml oil
- 100 g ground almonds or hazelnuts
- 1 tsp cinnamon
- 1 packet baking powder

Instructions:
Mix eggs, sugar, and oil. Fold in flour, baking powder, cinnamon, nuts, and carrots.
Pour into a greased pan and bake at 175°C (350°F) for 50–60 minutes.
Top with cream cheese frosting or powdered sugar.

Grießkuchen (Semolina Cake)

Ingredients:

- 1 liter milk
- 150 g semolina
- 100 g sugar
- 1 packet vanilla sugar
- 3 eggs
- Zest of 1 lemon

Instructions:
Bring milk to a boil, stir in semolina, sugar, and lemon zest.
Let cool slightly, then mix in eggs.
Pour into greased pan.
Bake at 180°C (350°F) for 35–40 minutes.
Dust with powdered sugar or serve with fruit sauce.

Vanillekuchen (Vanilla Cake)

Ingredients:

- 200 g butter
- 200 g sugar
- 4 eggs
- 250 g flour
- 1 packet baking powder
- 1 tbsp vanilla extract or 2 packets vanilla sugar
- 100 ml milk

Instructions:
Cream butter and sugar, add eggs and vanilla.
Fold in flour and baking powder, then milk.
Pour into loaf or round pan.
Bake at 175°C (350°F) for 50–60 minutes. Glaze or dust with sugar as desired.

Topfkuchen (Bundt Pan Cake)

Ingredients:

- 250 g butter
- 200 g sugar
- 1 packet vanilla sugar
- 4 eggs
- 300 g flour
- 1 packet baking powder
- 100 ml milk
- Optional: cocoa powder for marbled version

Instructions:

Cream butter, sugar, and vanilla sugar. Add eggs one at a time.
Mix in flour and baking powder, alternating with milk.
Optional: Divide batter and mix cocoa into half for marble effect.
Pour into greased Bundt pan and bake at 175°C (350°F) for 50–60 minutes.

Mandelkuchen (Almond Cake)

Ingredients:

- 250 g ground almonds
- 200 g sugar
- 4 eggs
- 100 g flour
- 1 packet baking powder
- Zest of 1 lemon
- Optional: 2–3 tbsp amaretto or almond liqueur

Instructions:
Beat eggs and sugar until light and fluffy.
Fold in almonds, flour, baking powder, and lemon zest.
Add liqueur if using.
Pour into a greased pan and bake at 175°C (350°F) for 40–50 minutes.
Dust with powdered sugar or glaze.

Johannisbeerkuchen (Red Currant Cake)

Ingredients:

- 200 g flour
- 100 g butter
- 75 g sugar
- 1 egg
- 300 g red currants
- 2 egg whites
- 100 g sugar

Instructions:
Prepare shortcrust dough, press into tart pan and prebake at 180°C (350°F) for 10 minutes.
Whip egg whites and sugar into stiff meringue.
Fold in red currants gently.
Spread over base and bake for another 20–25 minutes.

Puddingkuchen (Custard Pudding Cake)

Ingredients:

- **Base:** 200 g flour, 100 g butter, 1 egg, 75 g sugar

- **Filling:** 1 packet vanilla pudding, 500 ml milk, 2 tbsp sugar

- Optional: fruit layer (bananas, cherries, or peaches)

Instructions:
Make and chill base dough, press into springform.
Cook pudding, let cool slightly, then pour over base.
Add fruit if using.
Bake at 175°C (350°F) for 35–40 minutes. Chill before serving.

Zimtkuchen (Cinnamon Cake)

Ingredients:

- 250 g flour
- 150 g sugar
- 2 tsp cinnamon
- 1 packet baking powder
- 2 eggs
- 100 ml oil
- 150 ml milk

Instructions:
Mix dry ingredients, then add eggs, oil, and milk.
Pour into greased cake pan.
Bake at 180°C (350°F) for 35–40 minutes.
Optional: glaze with cinnamon icing or dust with powdered sugar.

Streusel-Mohn-Kuchen (Poppy Seed Crumble Cake)

Ingredients:

- **Base:** 250 g flour, 125 g butter, 1 egg, 75 g sugar

- **Filling:** 500 ml milk, 1 packet semolina or pudding powder, 100 g sugar, 200 g ground poppy seeds

- **Streusel:** 200 g flour, 100 g butter, 100 g sugar

Instructions:
Make crust and press into a pan.
Cook milk with sugar and pudding powder, stir in poppy seeds. Spread on base.
Top with streusel mixture.
Bake at 180°C (350°F) for 35–40 minutes.

Kirschtorte (Cherry Torte)

Ingredients:

- **Sponge:** 4 eggs, 150 g sugar, 150 g flour
- **Filling:** 1 jar sour cherries, 2 tbsp cornstarch, 2 tbsp sugar
- **Topping:** Whipped cream, chocolate shavings

Instructions:
Bake sponge in springform pan.
Drain cherries, cook with sugar and starch until thick.
Slice sponge horizontally.
Layer with cherry filling and whipped cream.
Top with whipped cream and chocolate shavings.

Eierkuchen (German Pancakes / Crêpes)

Ingredients:

- 250 g flour
- 3 eggs
- 500 ml milk
- 1 pinch salt
- Butter for frying

Instructions:
Whisk all ingredients into a smooth batter.
Let rest 10 minutes.
Heat butter in a pan and fry thin pancakes on both sides.
Serve with jam, cinnamon sugar, or applesauce.

Lebkuchenkuchen (Gingerbread Cake)

Ingredients:

- 250 g flour
- 150 g sugar
- 3 eggs
- 100 ml milk
- 100 g butter
- 1 packet baking powder
- 2 tbsp cocoa powder
- 2 tsp Lebkuchen spice (or mix of cinnamon, cloves, nutmeg, cardamom)

Instructions:
Mix all ingredients into a smooth batter.
Pour into a greased pan and bake at 175°C (350°F) for 30–40 minutes.
Optional: cover with chocolate glaze or icing.

Holunderblütenkuchen (Elderflower Cake)

Ingredients:

- 200 g butter
- 180 g sugar
- 4 eggs
- 250 g flour
- 1 packet baking powder
- 3–4 tbsp elderflower syrup
- Zest of 1 lemon
- Optional: glaze with elderflower syrup and powdered sugar

Instructions:

Cream butter and sugar, add eggs one at a time.
Mix in flour, baking powder, lemon zest, and elderflower syrup.
Pour into greased loaf pan.
Bake at 175°C (350°F) for 45–50 minutes.
Cool and glaze if desired.

Schokoladenkuchen (Chocolate Cake)

Ingredients:

- 200 g dark chocolate
- 200 g butter
- 200 g sugar
- 4 eggs
- 150 g flour
- 1 tsp baking powder

Instructions:
Melt chocolate and butter. Let cool slightly.
Beat eggs and sugar, stir in chocolate mixture.
Fold in flour and baking powder.
Pour into greased pan.
Bake at 180°C (350°F) for 35–40 minutes.
Top with chocolate glaze or dust with cocoa.

Käsesahnetorte (No-Bake Creamy Cheesecake Torte)

Ingredients:

- **Base:** 1 sponge cake layer or biscuit base

- **Filling:** 500 g Quark, 250 ml cream, 100 g sugar, 1 packet vanilla sugar, 6 sheets gelatin, juice of 1 lemon

Instructions:
Soften gelatin in cold water.
Whip cream. Mix Quark, sugar, lemon, and vanilla sugar.
Dissolve gelatin, mix with a little Quark mix, then stir all together.
Fold in whipped cream.
Pour on base in springform and chill for 4–6 hours.

Früchtebrotkuchen (Fruit Bread Cake)

Ingredients:

- 200 g dried fruits (figs, dates, raisins, apricots)
- 100 g chopped nuts
- 200 g flour
- 1 tsp baking powder
- 100 g brown sugar
- 2 eggs
- 1 tsp cinnamon
- 100 ml milk

Instructions:
Chop fruits and nuts.
Mix all ingredients into a dense batter.
Pour into a loaf pan.
Bake at 160°C (320°F) for 50–60 minutes.
Let cool, then optionally glaze with rum icing.

Rosinenkuchen (Raisin Cake)

Ingredients:

- 250 g flour
- 100 g sugar
- 125 g butter
- 2 eggs
- 100 g raisins (soaked in rum or water)
- 1 packet baking powder
- 100 ml milk

Instructions:
Cream butter and sugar, add eggs.
Mix in flour, baking powder, and milk.
Fold in raisins.
Pour into loaf or bundt pan.
Bake at 175°C (350°F) for 50–60 minutes.
Dust with powdered sugar.

Torte mit Baiser (Torte with Meringue)

Ingredients:

- **Base:** Sponge or shortcrust
- **Fruit layer:** berries, rhubarb, or cherries
- **Meringue:** 3 egg whites, 150 g sugar

Instructions:
Prepare base and prebake for 10 minutes.
Add fruit layer.
Whip egg whites and sugar to stiff peaks, spread or pipe over fruit.
Bake at 150°C (300°F) for another 20–25 minutes until meringue is golden.
Cool completely before slicing.

www.ingramcontent.com/pod-product-compliance
Lightning Source LLC
LaVergne TN
LVHW061950070526
838199LV00060B/4064